7 Keys to Activating

The Cyrus Anointing

By

Harold Herring

Debt Free Army
P.O. Box 900000, Fort Worth, TX 76161

7 Keys to Activating The Cyrus Anointing
By Harold Herring

ISBN 978-0-9763668-2-9
Copyright © 2014 by The Debt Free Army
P.O. Box 900000, Fort Worth, Texas 76161
817-222-0011
harold@haroldherring.com

v.1

Table of Contents

How to Get the Most Out of This Book   9

Why I Wrote This Book   17

What Is the Anointing?   21

Key # 1—God Will Bless Those Who Honor His Presence, His House and His Word   31

Key # 2—God Will Anoint and Equip You   39

Key # 3—God Will Go Before You to Protect You and Defeat Your Enemies   49

Key # 4—God Will Give You Hidden Treasures and Secret Riches   67

Key # 5—God Created and Called You for a Specific Purpose   77

Key # 6—God Will Raise You Up and Guide Your Actions   85

Key # 7—God Will Restore What the Enemy Has Taken From You   97

How Not to Activate the Cyrus Anointing   103

How to Activate the Cyrus Anointing Right Now   111

Prayer of Release for the Cyrus Anointing   127

Dedication

It's a real blessing to dedicate this book ... to one of the most anointed people I've ever met ... my Momma, Annie Ruth Herring.

"Ms." Annie Ruth, as she's known, has never written a book, pastored a church, spoken at large seminars or had her own television show ... but she has impacted thousands of lives ... the same way Jesus did ... one at a time and in small groups.

My Momma is one of the hardest working women I've ever known. She and my father operated businesses in our home town of LaGrange, North Carolina, for over 54 years.

Literally thousands of people were saved, delivered and healed because they walked into the businesses owned by my parents. In the past, local newspapers wrote articles about how their places of business were spiritual rest stops.

For nearly 60 years, my Momma has taught a

Sunday school class every week, and for the past nine plus years she has traveled to another church every Tuesday morning to teach a Bible study.

If you want to feel the presence of God, just say "Jesus" and listen as she tells of her love for Him ... and the power of His anointing.

I'm not dedicating this book to Ms. Annie Ruth just because she's my mother, but because she's an anointed woman of God, and everybody who's ever met her ... knows that's the truth.

One more thing, when recounting the miracles and moves of God in her life ... she will invariably say these words ... "You Ain't Seen Nothing Yet."

Thanks, Momma, for my Christian heritage.

How to Get the Most Out of This Book

First, get a pen or pencil.

If this book is to be a blessing to you ... nearly every page will have notes, asterisks, comments and ideas for practical implementation into your life.

Second, pray.

Ask God to help you grasp, comprehend, understand and activate every scriptural principle taught within the pages of this book ... so that the fruit of the time you invest ... will remain and produce a harvest ... for years to come.

John 15:16 says:

"Ye have not chosen me, but I have chosen you, and ordained you, that ye should go and bring

forth fruit, and that your fruit should remain: that whatsoever ye shall ask of the Father in my name, he may give it you."

The New Living Translation of John 15:16 says:

"You didn't choose me. I chose you. I appointed you to go and produce lasting fruit, so that the Father will give you whatever you ask for, using my name."

Now I want to show you how to personalize that verse ... by inserting your name directly inside.

"Harold didn't choose me. I chose him. I appointed him to go and produce lasting fruit, so that the Father will give Harold whatever he ask[s] for, using my name."

Now it's your turn to personalize John 15:16 ... changing the words that I underlined to reflect your name and gender.

> **Third, read the book without distraction.**

There may be some books that you can read while watching television ... this isn't one of them, or it shouldn't be.

THE CYRUS ANOINTING

If the room is filled with conversation from the family, either get a pair of ear plugs or put on some headphones.

This is not the occasion to listen to your favorite song climbing the Billboard charts. It's time for you to read without distraction what God has led me to put on these pages.

If you listen to music ... I recommend something instrumental and soothing. It's hard to hear what God is saying to you ... while listening to "Papa Was a Rolling Stone" by the Temptations or "Friends in Low Places" by Garth Brooks.

> **Fourth, read the book again, and this time use a yellow highlighter.**

Mark key phrases, sentences or thoughts that stir your faith.

There was a season in my life where I read a book a week. In fact, I accomplished that feat during eight years in a ten-year period. Each of those books was highlighted ... allowing me to quickly capture key nuggets and/or power thoughts from the words I had read.

> **Fifth, read this book utilizing a data retrieval system so you can record and later easily access the things you've read and written which will prompt a call to change in your life.**

I recommend these Rich Thoughts and action ideas be captured in a journal, laptop, iPad, smart phone or some other form of electronic recording and organizing system.

Truthfully, my notes are put into a drop box (i.e., dropbox.com) which makes them immediately accessible to all my electronic toys.

> **Sixth, don't delay in reflecting, recording and recalling the things that you've read and/or heard.**

It is a scientific fact that you will forget 50% of what you've read or heard within three hours of reading or hearing it. And sadly, twenty-four hours later you will have forgotten 50% of the remaining information.

By the end of 30 days, most people will recall less than 5% of that ... in other words only 2.5% of the original material that they were exposed to.

THE CYRUS ANOINTING

2 Timothy 2:15 says:

"Study to shew thyself approved unto God, a workman that needeth not to be ashamed, rightly dividing the word of truth."

The scripture says "study." It doesn't say "read once," "glance over," or "speed read through." The Word says "study," and I know the Holy Spirit used that Word for a reason.

Study is defined in dictionary.com as "application of the mind to the acquisition of knowledge, as by reading, investigation, or reflection."

As I read the definition of "study," it quickened in my spirit that the real process of "studying to show yourself approved" is contained in this definition.

Study is the acquisition of knowledge by reading, investigating and reflecting.

It's simple, really ... studying is a seed that you plant, and the harvest is knowledge that you acquire. In fact, the scripture says in Mark 4:24 in the Amplified Bible that you will receive back more than you sow.

"And He said to them, Be careful what you are hearing. The measure [of thought and study] you give [to the truth you hear] will be the measure

[of virtue and knowledge] that comes back to you—and more [besides] will be given to you who hear."

**Seventh, share what you've
read with a friend.**

In my opinion, when one believer meets another ... the first thing they should say after hello is ... "What has the Lord revealed to you since we last talked?"

When God reveals something to me in the Word, I'm anxious to share it with someone else. Why?

Proverbs 27:17 in the Contemporary English Version says:

"Just as iron sharpens iron, friends sharpen the minds of each other."

It's through this process that we can gain insight and deeper revelation in His Word ... about the decisions we need to make and the actions we need to take.

These seven keys are not just for this book ... but any other book God directs you to read.

Make no mistake ... God isn't interested in how

THE CYRUS ANOINTING

many books you can read or how fast you read them ... He simply wants to know if you *get it*.

Ready ... let's get ... started.

Why I Wrote This Book

Several years ago ... while reading about Queen Esther ... God brought to my attention ... the anointing on her son, King Cyrus.

I must confess that I didn't know that King Cyrus was the son of Queen Esther, nor did I know there was such a thing as a Cyrus Anointing.

I searched the scriptures ... did some historical research and I was ready to write, BUT (and it's a big BUT) God wasn't ready ...

His message to me was very clear ... WAIT.

> **I have now received a release from the Lord, and I know this is the time to write about the Cyrus Anointing and how it can be activated in your life.**

I wondered if God wanted me to write about the

first time King Cyrus is mentioned in the scripture.

2 Chronicles 36:22-23 says:

"Now in the first year of Cyrus king of Persia, that the word of the LORD spoken by the mouth of Jeremiah might be accomplished, the LORD stirred up the spirit of Cyrus king of Persia, that he made a proclamation throughout his entire kingdom, and put it also in writing, saying,

"Thus saith Cyrus king of Persia, All the kingdoms of the earth hath the LORD God of heaven given me; and he hath charged me to build him an house in Jerusalem, which is in Judah. Who is there among you of all his people? The LORD his God be with him, and let him go up."

While the verses were fascinating ... I immediately knew this was not what He wanted me to write about.

Next, I read the first three chapters of Ezra where King Cyrus captured Babylon and he freed the Jews to return home. Not only did he free the Jews in Ezra 1:7, he did something that showed his respect for their culture, heritage and possessions.

"Also Cyrus the king brought forth the vessels of the house of the LORD, which Nebuchadnezzar

THE CYRUS ANOINTING

had brought forth out of Jerusalem ..."

King Cyrus also provided all the necessary finances and materials for the rebuilding of Jerusalem, according to Ezra 3:7, which says:

> *"They gave money also unto the masons, and to the carpenters; and food, drink and oil to the Sidonians and the Tyrians, to bring cedar trees from Lebanon to the seaport of Joppa, according to the grant that they had from Cyrus king of Persia."*

But God didn't direct me to write about this either. Instead He led me to Isaiah 45. In the pages of this powerful book ... God revealed to me the seven keys to releasing the Cyrus Anointing in your life.

> **There is no question in my mind that this anointing is specifically for these end times.**

Before we look at the seven keys to operating in the Cyrus Anointing ...

... we should examine what the scripture has to say about His anointing.

What Is the Anointing?

When our youngest daughter Alexandra was about 4 years old ... she went to her room to take a nap. Within just a few moments, we heard her saying, "Ooooh Aaaah, only at Mattress Giant."

My purpose in telling you this story is not a social commentary on the effectiveness of television advertising in the lives of children and adults but rather what creates the "Ooooh Aaaah" feeling.

For many believers, the anointing is defined as witnessing events or supernatural moments that give them an "Ooooh Aaaah" feeling. The anointing is not restricted to such feelings ... because it's much more.

It's not unusual to hear people say, "He's so anointed," "She has a heavy anointing," "I can feel the healing anointing in the room," or even to hear them say, "I wish I operated in that kind of anointing."

I'm not minimizing people who make these statements or the manifestations of which they speak, but I'm saying that the anointing is much more than that. It's not limited to just the "Ooooh Aaaah" feelings.

How does the Word of God define the anointing?

John 14:26 in the Amplified Bible says:

"But the Comforter (Counselor, Helper, Intercessor, Advocate, Strengthener, Standby), the Holy Spirit, Whom the Father will send in My name [in My place, to represent Me and act on My behalf], He will teach you all things. And He will cause you to recall (will remind you of, bring to your remembrance) everything I have told you."

Let's look at the facts in this verse.

1. God is sending you the Holy Spirit ... which will counsel you, help you, pray for you, be an advocate for you, strengthen you and stand by you.

2. The Holy Spirit is sent to you to act, represent and act on behalf of Jesus.

John 5:20 in the Amplified Bible says:

"The Father dearly loves the Son and discloses

to (shows) Him everything that He Himself does. And He will disclose to Him (let Him see) greater things yet than these, so that you may marvel and be full of wonder and astonishment."

John 14:12 in the Amplified Bible says:

"I assure you, most solemnly I tell you, if anyone steadfastly believes in Me, he will himself be able to do the things that I do; and he will do even greater things than these, because I go to the Father."

3. You will know all things ... meaning ... there's nothing you won't know.

4. You will be able to remember everything He has taught you.

Now let's go a little further.

> **The Holy Spirit is not an it or a thing but rather the third person of the Trinity (Father, Son and Holy Spirit).**

Now, the question arises, how does the Holy Spirit function through you?

1 John 2:20 says:

"But ye have an unction from the Holy One, and ye know all things."

According to Strong's Concordance the Greek word for unction is chrisma (G5545) and it means:

"... anything smeared on, unguent, ointment, usually prepared by the Hebrews from oil and aromatic herbs."

1 John 2:27 says:

"But the anointing which ye have received of him abideth in you, and ye need not that any man teach you: but as the same anointing teacheth you of all things, and is truth, and is no lie, and even as it hath taught you, ye shall abide in him."

According to the Strong's Concordance the Greek word for anointing is the exact same word used for unction found in 1 John 2:20.

The word "chrisma" comes from the root word chriō (G5548) which means:

"... to anoint; consecrating Jesus to the Messianic office, and furnishing him with the necessary powers for its administration **and enduing Christians with the gifts of the Holy Spirit**."

THE CYRUS ANOINTING

The word chriō (G5548) appears five times in the Greek Concordance of the King James Version.

Luke 4:18 says:

"The Spirit of the Lord is upon me, because he hath anointed me to preach the gospel to the poor; he hath sent me to heal the brokenhearted, to preach deliverance to the captives, and recovering of sight to the blind, to set at liberty them that are bruised."

Some people read this verse and say that the anointing only applies to people who are preaching the gospel ... ministers ... preachers ... evangelists. Not true.

In Strong's Concordance *"to preach the gospel"* is the Greek word *"euaggelizō"* (G2097) and it means:

"... to bring good news, to announce glad tidings."

I have a revelation for you ... you don't have to be an ordained minister of the gospel to bring good news ... you just need to be anointed ... with power, wisdom and insight from the Holy Spirit.

Luke 4:18 also says that we're to "preach deliverance to the captives." The Greek word for preach is kēryssō (G2784) and it means:

"... to proclaim in the manner of a herald; to publish, proclaim openly: something which has been done."

You don't have to have an ordination certificate hanging on your wall to publish and proclaim the deliverance found in the Word of God.

The captives are set free ... not because of someone's education ... but because of the anointing.

Isaiah 10:27 says:

"And it shall come to pass in that day, that his burden shall be taken away from off thy shoulder, and his yoke from off thy neck, and the yoke shall be destroyed because of the anointing."

Let's look at Luke 4:18 in the New Living Translation which says:

"The Spirit of the Lord is upon me, for he has anointed me to bring Good News to the poor. He has sent me to proclaim that captives will be released, that the blind will see, that the oppressed will be set free."

If the Spirit of the Lord is upon you, and it is ...

then YOU have been anointed to bring the Good News to the poor.

What's the best news you can bring to the poor ... you don't have to live that way anymore.

What's the best news you can proclaim to the captives of debt and lack ... you don't have to live that way anymore.

What's the best news you can bring to the blind ... now you can see; the Word of God gives you a way of escape from all that has had you bound.

What's the best news you can bring to the oppressed ... you're free.

Acts 10:38 in the Amplified Bible says:

"How God anointed and consecrated Jesus of Nazareth with the [Holy] Spirit and with strength and ability and power; how He went about doing good and, in particular, curing all who were harassed and oppressed by [the power of] the devil, for God was with Him."

1. God anoints you with the Holy Spirit.

2. The Holy Spirit gives you strength, ability and power ... beyond even what you thought

possible or yourself capable of.

3. You're anointed to do good ... to bless and help others.

4. God will use you to bring inward and outward healing.

5. The Message translation of Acts 10:38 says that you will bring "... healing [to] everyone ... beaten down by the Devil."

6. God will be with you ... as you operate in the anointing of the Holy Spirit.

Always remember, you will never really be free until you are financially free.

You've gotta love the last part of Luke 4:18 in The Message when it says:

"... To set the burdened and battered free, to announce, 'This is God's year to act!' "

This is your year ... this is your time to act ... to operate under His anointing.

Amos 9:13 in the Amplified Bible says:

"Behold, the days are coming, says the Lord,

that the plowman shall overtake the reaper, and the treader of grapes him who sows the seed; and the mountains shall drop sweet wine and all the hills shall melt [that is, everything heretofore barren and unfruitful shall overflow with spiritual blessing]."

The Message translation of Amos 9:13 says:

" 'Yes indeed, it won't be long now.' God's Decree. 'Things are going to happen so fast your head will swim, one thing fast on the heels of the other. You won't be able to keep up. Everything will be happening at once—and everywhere you look, blessings! Blessings like wine pouring off the mountains and hills. I'll make everything right again for my people Israel.' "

This is your year ... to operate in His anointing ... and yes, the end-time Cyrus Anointing.

Key # 1 ...

To the Cyrus Anointing

God Will Bless Those Who Honor Him, His House and His Word.

Cyrus was the great king and conqueror of his day. But he understood the value of giving to God what belonged to God.

Isaiah 45:1 in the New Living Translation says:

"This is what the LORD says to Cyrus, his anointed one, whose right hand he will empower ..."

Most conquering leaders would have kept the booty they found in Babylon but not King Cyrus. There was never hesitation in his decision to return to Israel the treasures from the Temple in Jerusalem.

Ezra 6:5 says:

"And also let the golden and silver vessels of the house of God, which Nebuchadnezzar took forth out of the Temple which is at Jerusalem, and brought unto Babylon, be restored, and brought again unto the Temple which is at Jerusalem, everyone to his place, and place them in the house of God."

> **King Cyrus honored God ... and that's exactly what we should do.**

How do we honor God? One way for sure is to follow the instructions in the owner's manual.

We don't call the Bible an owner's manual, but that is essentially what it is for us.

I have discovered that instruction manuals ... while I may not understand them at first ... while I might complain because they just don't make sense ... while I'm frustrated over my inability to figure them out ... are valuable if I persevere. I soon realize that the instruction manual contains the answers I need. I find them helpful and much easier to understand than I had first thought.

THE CYRUS ANOINTING

There are some folks ... who are not getting real answers to the real problems they're facing in life because they're trying to put their lives together without the benefit of their instruction manual.

Some folks have decided the instruction manual for successful living is too difficult to read or understand, so they ignore it or only give it a casual glance in the midst of adversity.

Our manufacturer created an instruction manual for each of us to survive and thrive in any and every situation, circumstance and problem we face in life. However, here's a revelation ... if we don't read and study it, then we'll continually have problems all the days of our natural born life.

2 Timothy 3:16-17 says:

"All scripture is given by inspiration of God, and is profitable for doctrine, for reproof, for correction, for instruction in righteousness: That the man of God may be perfect, thoroughly furnished unto all good works."

If something is profitable ... it's going to be beneficial. The word *profitable* in the Strong's Concordance is from a Greek word that means **"profitable, advantage."**

If we want to have advantages in life then we need to understand our instruction manual ... God's Holy Word. Every answer to every problem we face is in the book.

The Bible ... our instruction manual ... is an incredible tool for handling every single area of our life.

Let me give you four reasons why you should read your instruction manual.

> **First, the manual will bring stability into your life regardless of what type of personal turbulence you may be experiencing.**

Ephesians 4:14 in the Amplified Bible says:

"So then, we may no longer be children, tossed [like ships] to and fro between chance gusts of teaching and wavering with every changing wind of doctrine, [the prey of] the cunning and cleverness of unscrupulous men, [gamblers engaged] in every shifting form of trickery in inventing errors to mislead."

> **Second, read the instruction manual because He said to.**

THE CYRUS ANOINTING

PERIOD. PARAGRAPH.

1 Timothy 4:13 says:

"Till I come, give attendance to reading, to ex-hortation, to doctrine."

If the Word of God ... our instruction manual ... tells us to do something ... then we JUST DO IT.

According to 1 Timothy 4:15 in The Message, we're not just to read the instruction manual ... we're to saturate ourselves in His Word.

"Cultivate these things. Immerse yourself in them. The people will all see you mature right before their eyes!"

> **Third, read the manual because truth builds upon truth.**

2 Timothy 3:14-15 in the Amplified Bible says:

"But as for you, continue to hold to the things that you have learned and of which you are con-vinced, knowing from whom you learned [them], and how from your childhood you have had a knowledge of and been acquainted with the sa-cred Writings, which are able to instruct you and

give you the understanding for salvation which comes through faith in Christ Jesus [through the leaning of the entire human personality on God in Christ Jesus in absolute trust and confidence in His power, wisdom, and goodness]."

Fourth, read the manual to understand the gifts your Heavenly Father wants to give you.

---

1 Corinthians 12:1 says:

"Now concerning spiritual gifts, brethren, I would not have you ignorant."

God does not want you ignorant about every blessing, benefit and gift that He has waiting for you ... other translations say that He does not want us "misinformed" or for us to "misunderstand" what He's providing to us.

The only way you know what God has in store for you ... is to read the instruction manual. Now to me, that just seems like good common sense.

In reading, studying and acting on the instruction manual ... we will do what He does.

THE CYRUS ANOINTING

Ephesians 5:1 in the New Living Translation says:

"[Living in the Light] Imitate God, therefore, in everything you do, because you are his dear children."

On a daily basis you and I should desire that every step we take ... every word we speak ... bring glory and honor to Him. Our concern should be to represent His Godly character because we are His dear children.

1 Peter 4:11 in the New Living Translation says:

"Do you have the gift of speaking? Then speak as though God himself were speaking through you. Do you have the gift of helping others? Do it with all the strength and energy that God supplies. Then everything you do will bring glory to God through Jesus Christ. All glory and power to him forever and ever! Amen."

Everything we do should bring honor and glory to Him.

Key # 2 ...

To the Cyrus Anointing

God Will Anoint and Equip You.

When you do what's right before the Lord ... when you're called by God to fulfill His purpose ... He will anoint and equip you.

In Isaiah 44:28 the Amplified Bible says:

"Who says of Cyrus, He is My shepherd (ruler), and he shall perform all My pleasure and fulfill all My Purpose—even saying of Jerusalem, She shall [again] be built, and of the temple, Your foundation shall [again] be laid."

As a result of Cyrus' willingness to be used for God's glory He was anointed and empowered.

HAROLD HERRING

Isaiah 45:1 in The Message says:

"God's Message to his anointed, to Cyrus ..."

God wants to empower (equip) you ... this is not through some bodybuilding course or a daily trip to a 24-hour fitness center.

Ephesians 3:16 in the New Living Translation says:

"I pray that from his glorious, unlimited resources he will empower you with inner strength through his Spirit."

I know that some of you, as you're reading these words, are wondering whether or not God will anoint and empower you. The answer is: YES, HE WILL.

The real question is not whether God will empower you, but who and what are *you* empowering?

I'm going to ask you some questions, and I want you to make sure your answers are honest ... because God will know whether or not you're telling the truth.

Are your debt problems just as serious as your unsaved neighbor's ... if so, what kind of testimony is that?

Are you unable to keep a job ... if so, what kind

of testimony is that?

Do you get mad when someone cuts in front of you on the freeway and then treat them just like the next guy ... if so, what kind of testimony is that?

Do you curse and tell dirty jokes just like your lost co-workers ... if so, what kind of testimony is that?

If your yard is filled with weeds and your house is in disrepair just like your neighbor's ... if so, what kind of testimony is that?

If you watch "R" rated movies filled with nudity and 4-letter words just like your neighbor ... if so, what kind of testimony is that?

Consider the words of Colossians 3:17 which say:

"And whatsoever ye do in word or deed, do all in the name of the Lord Jesus, giving thanks to God and the Father by him."

In other words, if we live and act just like our unsaved neighbors, co-workers and acquaintances ... what kind of testimony are we for the Lord?

If we act like them ... then we don't have to worry about the Cyrus Anointing, as it will never be released into our lives.

Whatever we do ...

... should glorify God.

Matthew 5:13 says that we're to be the salt of the earth.

"Ye are the salt of the earth: but if the salt hath lost his savour, wherewith shall it be salted? It is thenceforth good for nothing, but to be cast out, and to be trodden under foot of men."

I love The Message translation of Matthew 5:13:

"Let me tell you why you are here. You're here to be salt-seasoning that brings out the God-flavors of this earth. If you lose your saltiness, how will people taste godliness? You've lost your usefulness and will end up in the garbage."

A dear friend of this ministry ... Pam from Valrico, Florida, told me once that we should be SALT. She gave one of the most powerful and appropriate acronyms of SALT that I've ever heard.

THE CYRUS ANOINTING

S ... Stop

A ... Acting

L ... Like

T ... Them

We're to stop acting like the world. There should be a discernable difference in the words we speak ... the actions we take and the testimony of the things that we've said and done ... because of who we are in Christ.

Now let's go a little further.

Have you ever heard the old expression "money talks"?

My standard joke used to be, if "money talked," for most of my life it was saying good-bye ... either that or I needed a hearing aid. So much for the humor ... now let's get serious, because once I got serious, money started coming to me.

I want you to think very carefully about this next statement.

Your money does "talk" ... it makes an impression. Whatever you give money to ... you empower.

If you give your money to buy Hostess Twinkies ... then you're empowering the Hostess Brands, LLC bakery company.

If you buy homeowners or automobile insurance ... then you're empowering an insurance company.

If you buy a Mountain Dew soft drink ... then you're empowering the Pepsi Corporation.

If you purchase a Chevrolet Malibu ... then you're empowering GM, the General Motors Corporation.

If you buy things from companies that disrespect Christian values or support things you oppose ... then you are empowering those companies.

Let me digress for a second.

If we watch television programming that vilifies biblical principles ... then we are empowering that network to continue its attack on our core values as Christians.

I will tell you that my fine wife Bev is a "Christian pit bull." When something is said or done during a television show that stirs her righteous indignation, she will fire off an email, make a phone call and not likely watch that television program again.

I realize that the majority of the television and motion picture industry is run by people who not only don't understand the scriptures but seemingly have no desire to hear or represent any other viewpoint other than their own ungodly one.

Nevertheless, that shouldn't stop us from speaking up in "word and deed" whenever and wherever we feel there is scriptural injustice or inaccuracy. If every believer let their voices be heard ... it would make a difference.

If there is one thing the movie *The Passion of the Christ* proved ... it's that there's a market for movies that appeal to Christians. There has been a discernable increase in the number of theatrical releases that promote Christian values, and they've done remarkably well at the box office.

> **Never assume that your voice won't be heard ... that your opinion won't count. It's time for every believer to speak up in "word and deed."**

Now let's get back to the money aspect of this teaching.

> **Whatever you do with your money is a testimony to your "words and deeds."**

Do you spend more money on movie rentals than you do buying CDs that can transform your life by changing the way you think?

By the way, I didn't make up that last phrase. It's scripture.

Romans 12:2 in the New Living Translation says:

"Let God transform you by changing the way you think."

Matthew 12:34 in the Amplified Bible says:

"... For out of the fullness (the overflow, the superabundance) of the heart the mouth speaks."

The scripture in Colossians 3:17 says we should glorify God in our *"words and deeds."*

If we closely examine Matthew 12:34-37 in The

THE CYRUS ANOINTING

Message translation ... we can see the consequences of what will happen if we don't obey His directions.

> *"You have minds like a snake pit! How do you suppose what you say is worth anything when you are so foul-minded? It's your heart, not the dictionary, that gives meaning to your words. A good person produces good deeds and words season after season. An evil person is a blight on the orchard. Let me tell you something: Every one of these careless words is going to come back to haunt you. There will be a time of Reckoning. Words are powerful; take them seriously. Words can be your salvation. Words can also be your damnation."*

Let's look at a couple of key phrases ...

> *"It's your heart, not the dictionary, that gives meaning to your words."*

Remember Matthew 12:34 says that out of the abundance of the heart the mouth speaks.

A good person, because of the good things in his or her heart, will do the right thing year in and year out.

> *"A good person produces good deeds and words season after season."*

We should pay attention to this next Power Verse excerpt taken from Matthew 12:34-37:

> *"Every one of these careless words is going to come back to haunt you ... Words are powerful; take them seriously. Words can be your salvation. Words can also be your damnation."*

> **Every word we speak ... every step we take ... everything we do ... either empowers our spiritual life or weakens it.**

God has given us the key ... it's time for us to follow His Word ... not the world.

I've focused on being equipped and empowered in this chapter because so much more has been written about being anointed.

However, I do feel led to offer one final observation.

I very strongly believe that the anointing of God does not transfer simply because of the family a person is born into. It's not genetics but character and calling that determine the anointing in which a person walks.

Key # 3 ...

To the Cyrus Anointing

God Will Go Before You to Protect You and Defeat Your Enemies.

Isaiah 45:1-2 in the Amplified Bible says:

"... I will unarm and ungird the loins of kings to open the doors before him, so that gates will not be shut. I will go before you and level the mountains [to make the crooked places straight]; I will break into pieces the doors of bronze and cut asunder the bars of iron."

What God did for King Cyrus ... He will do for you ... since He's no respecter of persons (Acts 10:34).

Debt is your enemy ... lack is your enemy ...

49

sickness is your enemy ... when you've committed your life to God's purpose ... when you're sowing seeds for the building of His temple ... His body ... then you can walk in His divine protection.

Exodus 23:23 in the New Living Translation says:

"For my angel will go before you and bring you into the land of the Amorites, Hittites, Perizzites, Canaanites, Hivites, and Jebusites, so you may live there. And I will destroy them completely."

The Ammonite Spirit is a false voice ... one that is accusing and speaking against you.

The Hittite Spirit is one of dread and fear.

The Perizzite Spirit is a squatter spirit ... one without walls ... that will seek to dispossess you from what belongs to you.

The Canaanite Spirit wants to keep you mentally depressed, financially busted and without hope.

The Hivite Spirit is one of wickedness and deception.

The Jebusite Spirit is one of heaviness, negativity ... of being trampled down.

THE CYRUS ANOINTING

Exodus 34:10-12 in The Message says:

"And God said, 'As of right now, I'm making a covenant with you: In full sight of your people I will work wonders that have never been created in all the Earth, in any nation. Then all the people with whom you're living will see how tremendous God's work is, the work I'll do for you. Take careful note of all I command you today. I'm clearing your way by driving out Amorites, Canaanites, Hittites, Perizzites, Hivites, and Jebusites. Stay vigilant. Don't let down your guard lest you make covenant with the people who live in the land that you are entering and they trip you up.' "

Deuteronomy 1:21 in the New Living Translation says:

"Look! He has placed the land in front of you. Go and occupy it as the LORD, the God of your ancestors, has promised you. Don't be afraid! Don't be discouraged!"

We're entitled to the same blessings as the children of Israel ... we are heirs to the promises ... the covenant God made with our forefathers. His desire is for us to march out of Egypt (debt) and into the Promised Land (financial independence).

God promises to accompany us on our journey if

we obey His instructions and stay faithfully on the right path. The children of Israel had to deal with the six peoples (spirits) listed in Exodus 34:10. Each sought to prevent them from activating the covenant promises of God.

It's time for you to expose and deal with these six spirits whose purpose is to hinder you from entering your Promised Land. If you're dealing with financial stress ... it can be traced back to these six spirits.

> **First, the Canaanite Spirit wants to keep you mentally depressed, financially busted and without hope**.

The ultimate intent is to keep you from achieving what God has planned for you. This spirit wants you humiliated by debt and addicted to the spirit of greed ... a spirit which likes to keep people from receiving their rightful inheritance.

It's time to get real.

Every time you spend less than you earn, follow your budget/spending plan, refuse to fall for seductive advertising ... you fend off the spirit of greed that's circling you like a hawk about to make a dive for your wallet or credit cards.

THE CYRUS ANOINTING

The spirit of greed knows how to entice your flesh to buy "stuff" that you don't need and may not even be able to afford.

Greed is addictive ... it has an insatiable appetite, and its end game is to humiliate you financially. With God's help you need to break the spirit of greed out of your life ... along with the spirit of debt and lack.

I'm always amazed that the children of Israel developed a "what's in it for me" attitude on their journey from bondage to freedom. Talk about ingratitude. Every time their circumstances wavered, so did their faith.

The enemy will do what he can to lure you back to a lifestyle of debt and lack. He wants you looking to everything and everybody else but God.

Deuteronomy 7:25-26 in The Message translation says:

"Make sure you set fire to their carved gods. Don't get greedy for the veneer of silver and gold on them and take it for yourselves—you'll get trapped by it for sure. GOD hates it; it's an abomination to GOD, your God. And don't dare bring one of these abominations home or you'll end up just like it, burned up as a holy destruction. No: It is forbidden! Hate it. Abominate it. Destroy it and preserve GOD's holiness."

Galatians 5:16 in the New Living Translation says:

"So I say, let the Holy Spirit guide your lives. Then you won't be doing what your sinful nature craves."

Galatians 6:7 in the Amplified Bible says:

"Do not be deceived and deluded and misled; God will not allow Himself to be sneered at (scorned, disdained, or mocked by mere pretensions or professions, or by His precepts being set aside.) [He inevitably deludes himself who attempts to delude God.] For whatever a man sows, that and that only is what he will reap."

Proverbs 6:31 promises that if the thief be found, he must repay sevenfold. We can claim seven ideas for every idea the devil steals from us. Our prayers bind and cancel every attack against us in Jesus' name.

> **Second, the Hittite Spirit is one of dread and fear.**

As a child of God and rightful heir to a financial inheritance ... you've got to know that the enemy will try to tempt you ... spiritually, emotionally and physically to get you off track.

The enemy has no power over a born again believer, but he does have three abilities ... the ability to deceive, accuse and tempt. The enemy realizes that if he can cloud your mind with insecurity, doubt and fear ... then he can entrap you into a lifestyle of lack.

If you check the caller ID before answering every phone call to determine whether or not a bill collector is calling ... then you're living in fear and doubt. If you pray before opening the mailbox while dreading more past-due bills, then you know what I'm talking about.

Fear and dread ... don't want to leave your life ... they desire to be your constant companion ... however, you've got the Word and the power over every attack of the enemy. You must continue to resist this spirit, and it will have to flee. When it comes back, make it plain that it is not welcome and can no longer torment you.

Stand strong, and it will have to leave.

We are not to have ...
... the spirit of fear.

Romans 8:15 in the New English Translation says:

"For you did not receive the spirit of slavery lead-

ing again to fear, but you received the Spirit of adoption, by whom we cry, 'Abba, Father.' "

According to the Word of God we don't have to live in dread ... because we live in hope of His glory. Quote scripture to fear until it leaves you alone.

Romans 5:5 in the Amplified Bible says:

"Such hope never disappoints or deludes or shames us, for God's love has been poured out in our hearts through the Holy Spirit Who has been given to us."

Trusting in God's plan for your finances takes you out of hopelessness. The Hittite spirit wants to entrap you mentally. When you are bombarded with negatives ... start rejoicing.

First, it means you are breaking free, or the spirit would not be telling you, "You can't!"

Second, God inhabits the praises of His people, and the spirit of dread and fear cannot stay in that environment.

God will never disappoint you regardless of your financial circumstances. Remember, Joseph was in the prison one day, and the next he was in the palace.

THE CYRUS ANOINTING

> **Third, the Ammonite Spirit is a false voice ... one that is accusing and speaking against you.**

Revelation 12:10, 11 says:

"And I heard a loud voice saying in heaven, Now is come salvation, and strength, and the kingdom of our God, and the power of his Christ: for the accuser of our brethren is cast down, which accused them before our God day and night.

"And they overcame him by the blood of the Lamb, and by the word of their testimony; and they loved not their lives unto the death."

Scripture confirms we do have an adversary to contend with ... and without God he will devour us.

1 Peter 5:8 says:

"Be sober, be vigilant; because your adversary the devil, as a roaring lion, walketh about, seeking whom he may devour."

The enemy will seek to destroy your finances so he can render you ineffective for the Kingdom of God.

The enemy will tempt you into making unwise purchases ... he will deceive you into believing you can afford the purchase ... but once you've messed up ... he will accuse you of not having any will power ... trying to convince you that there is NO way out of your situation.

The devil cannot devour the faithful in Christ Jesus. Those who flatly resist him as the Bible directs, cannot be touched by the devil.

1 Corinthians 10:13 says:

"There hath no temptation taken you but such as is common to man: but God is faithful, who will not suffer you to be tempted above that ye are able; but will with the temptation also make a way to escape, that ye may be able to bear it."

Those who battle with the devil as children of God are more than conquerors (Romans 8:37).

We can defeat him every time he tries to slither into our lives.

The only way the enemy will defeat you financially or any other way is if you allow him to. The devil can't destroy your future once you dismiss his presence in your past.

THE CYRUS ANOINTING

Luke 10:18-20 in The Message says:

"Jesus said, 'I know. I saw Satan fall, a bolt of lightning out of the sky. See what I've given you? Safe passage as you walk on snakes and scorpions, and protection from every assault of the Enemy. No one can put a hand on you. All the same, the great triumph is not in your authority over evil, but in God's authority over you and presence with you. Not what you do for God but what God does for you—that's the agenda for rejoicing.' "

> **Fourth, the Perizzite Spirit is a squatter spirit ... one without walls ... that will seek to dispossess you from what belongs to you.**

It's generally a lack of discipline that opens a person to this type of attack.

Unfortunately, when it comes to financial planning even on a daily basis ... most people lack control over their money, and for that matter, their lives.

Sadly, we're witnessing an unprecedented surge in bankruptcies, ruined credit reports and foreclosures. There was a time when people were prudent about managing their finances, but now they spend more time juggling their payments and credit card balances.

I want you to write down this next sentence and repeat it over and over until it becomes engrafted in you.

"My financial destiny is directly affected by how I manage my money today."

When it comes to financial discipline ... it's taught at home ... one way or another. Children will either learn to save, refuse impulse buying and emotional spending ... or they will face continual financial ruin.

Most people who end up in financial trouble have not realized that saying "no" to spending is saying "yes" to a better, peaceful and more financially successful future.

Lack of discipline in any area of life will shorten and diminish what could have been ... it will rob your spiritual inheritance from under your nose. Short term gratification should never be traded for long-term financial success.

Job 5:17 in the New Living Translation says:

"But consider the joy of those corrected by God! Do not despise the discipline of the Almighty

when you sin."

> **Fifth, the Hivite Spirit is one of wickedness and deception.**

The children of Israel were deceived into taking their eyes off God just because things weren't going the way they planned. They reverted to rebellion and trusted their own timing, their understanding of how things should go. Like children they looked to what had been comfortable in the past, not to the promise of the future.

As long as things were easy and God was miraculously moving them ahead, they would follow. But if their journey slowed a pace or two, so did their faith.

We may go through a financial test of faith and turn to God for answers. If we hear a good sermon on stewardship or if the economy takes a dive, we head for spiritual safety and beg God for help. When things balance out and we gain a financial hold, we turn again to trust in our own abilities.

Truth is, good circumstances are only an illusion of security, and bad circumstances are only an illusion of insecurity. Trusting in what we see or feel is standing on shaky ground. Standing on the Word is rock solid.

We cannot be swayed by daily circumstances.

Romans 8:28 in the New Living Translation says:

"And we know that God causes everything to work together for the good of those who love God and are called according to his purpose for them."

Romans 4:21 in the New International Version says:

"... being fully persuaded that God had power to do what he had promised."

> **Sixth, the Jebusite Spirit is one of heaviness, negativity, of being trampled down.**

Debt is evil ... strangling God's purpose and potential out of our lives causing us to become slaves to the bondage of debt.

Debt leaves a legacy of defeat and impotence while it squanders the potential success and effectiveness of your life as a Christian.

And, after all, isn't that exactly what the enemy wants ... he offers the enticement of better things only to leave you in the desert looking around for anything that has any power to sustain your life.

Stop the working of the Spirit of Debt now. Follow me, and we will build your prosperity one day, and then another day, until you are debt free.

Deuteronomy 1:21 in the New Living Translation says:

"Look! He has placed the land in front of you. Go and occupy it as the LORD, the God of your ancestors, has promised you. Don't be afraid! Don't be discouraged!"

Are you ready to enter into a new dimension of your covenant with your Heavenly Father?

Consider the words again of Exodus 34:10-12 in The Message:

"And God said, 'As of right now, I'm making a covenant with you: In full sight of your people I will work wonders that have never been created in all the Earth, in any nation. Then all the people with whom you're living will see how tremendous God's work is, the work I'll do for you. Take careful note of all I command you today. I'm clearing your way by driving out Amorites, Canaanites,

Hittites, Perizzites, Hivites, and Jebusites. Stay vigilant. Don't let down your guard lest you make covenant with the people who live in the land that you are entering and they trip you up.' "

Matthew 11:28-30 in the Amplified Bible says:

"Come to Me, all you who labor and are heavy-laden and overburdened, and I will cause you to rest. [I will ease and relieve and refresh your souls.] Take My yoke upon you and learn of Me, for I am gentle (meek) and humble (lowly) in heart, and you will find rest (relief and ease and refreshment and recreation and blessed quiet) for your souls. For My yoke is wholesome (useful, good--not harsh, hard, sharp, or pressing, but comfortable, gracious, and pleasant), and My burden is light and easy to be borne."

God is ready to do tremendous work in and for you ... He will clear out all the "-ites" but you must stay vigilant ... don't let down your guard ... don't get lured into debt or unwise expenditures ... put Him first ... He will clear a path for you ... on your journey to the debt-free lifestyle.

Now it's time to shout ... read, study and mediate on Psalm 139:1-6 in The Message, which says:

"God, investigate my life; get all the facts

THE CYRUS ANOINTING

firsthand. I'm an open book to you; even from a distance, you know what I'm thinking. <u>You know when I leave and when I get back; I'm never out of your sight</u>. You know everything I'm going to say before I start the first sentence. <u>I look behind me and you're there, then up ahead and you're there, too—your reassuring presence, coming and going</u>. This is too much, too wonderful—I can't take it all in!"

Please study Verse 3 and Verse 5 which I have underlined ... get these passages down in your spirit.

Key # 4 ...

To the Cyrus Anointing

**God Will Give You Hidden
Treasures and Secret Riches.**

Isaiah 45:3 in the New Living Translation says:

*"And I will give you treasures hidden in the dark-
ness—secret riches. I will do this so you may
know that I am the Lord, the God of Israel, the
one who calls you by name."*

Job 28:11 in God's Word Translation says:

*"They explore the sources of rivers so that they
bring hidden treasures to light."*

The Word of the Lord wants you to know ... your

Heavenly Father is going to give you treasures and riches from places you'd never expect. He is going to create flowing wealth in your life so that He can be glorified.

2 Corinthians 9:10-11 in the New Living Translation says:

"For God is the one who provides seed for the farmer and then bread to eat. In the same way, he will provide and increase your resources and then produce a great harvest of generosity in you. Yes, you will be enriched in every way so that you can always be generous. And when we take your gifts to those who need them, they will thank God."

Even though God will give you hidden treasures and secret riches ... the path to this prosperity is clearly spelled out in the scripture.

Proverbs 11:24 says:

"There is that scattereth, and yet increaseth; and there is that withholdeth more than is meet, but it tendeth to poverty."

The Contemporary English Version of Proverbs 11:24 says:

"... you can become rich by being generous or

poor by being greedy."

"Giving to increase" is totally contrary to natural logic and human reasoning which says that if you give away something, then it's gone forever.

There are 12 benefits of being generous ... and I want to share them with you.

1. To expand your horizon and increase your opportunities, then you must be a giver.

Proverbs 11:24 in The Message says:

"The world of the generous gets larger and larger; the world of the stingy gets smaller and smaller."

2. A generous giver is blessed in everything he or she does.

Deuteronomy 15:10 in the New Living Translation says:

"Give generously to the poor, not grudgingly, for the Lord your God will bless you in everything you do."

The Message translation of Deuteronomy 15:10-11 says it this way:

"Give freely and spontaneously. Don't have a

stingy heart. The way you handle matters like this triggers God, your God's, blessing in every-thing you do, all your work and ventures. There are always going to be poor and needy people among you. So I command you: Always be gen-erous, open purse and hands, give to your neighbors in trouble, your poor and hurting neighbors."

3. Generosity is the best way to get through diffi-cult times.

How do you see your way through a financial crisis or economic turndown?

Psalm 112:4 in the New Living Translation says:

"Light shines in the darkness for the godly. They are generous, compassionate, and righteous."

4. When everyone else is getting bad news from their employer, the news media or Wall Street ... those who are generous are getting good news.

Psalm 112:5 in the New Living Translation says:

"Good comes to those who lend money gener-ously and conduct their business fairly."

5. There is only one way to limit the money coming

into your hand ... and it has nothing to do with your circumstances, situations or problems.

2 Corinthians 9:6 in the New Living Translation says:

"Remember this—a farmer who plants only a few seeds will get a small crop. But the one who plants generously will get a generous crop. Anything that you hold tightly in your hand ... will never be released to become a blessing."

The scripture is clear: a person who does not give generously ... one who, because of the current financial uncertainty, holds onto what they perceive to be all they have ... will only find greater economic distress.

6. **There is only one way for a fresh wind to blow in your finances.**

Proverbs 11:25 in the New Living Translation says:

"The generous will prosper; those who refresh others will themselves be refreshed."

7. **Generosity guarantees that your needs will be met ... and that you will have enough left over to bless others.**

2 Corinthians 9:8 in the New Living Translation says:

"And God will generously provide all you need. Then you will always have everything you need and plenty left over to share with others."

Notice this verse says "… you will always have." It doesn't say you might have, you could have, you should have … no, it says: *"YOU WILL ALWAYS HAVE EVERYTHING YOU NEED AND PLENTY LEFT OVER …"*

8. **When you are generous YOU WILL ALWAYS HAVE EVERYTHING YOU NEED AND PLENTY LEFT OVER.**

2 Corinthians 9:11 in the New Living Translation says:

"Yes, you will be enriched in every way so that you can always be generous …"

Once again, the scripture says, "YOU WILL be enriched in every way."

The scripture doesn't say some ways … a few ways … no, it says EVERY WAY.

Why do you and I have money? Is it to buy stuff?

Is it to keep up with the Joneses? Is it to invest for our retirement? Why does God give us "the power to get wealth"?

God is the ultimate giver. He will be sure we receive in response to how we provide those good things for others.

1 Timothy 6:18 in the New Living Translation says:

"Tell them to use their money to do good. They should be rich in good works and generous to those in need, always being ready to share with others."

9. Generosity makes a person a devout believer.

Acts 10:2 in the New Living Translation says:

"He was a devout, God-fearing man, as was everyone in his household. He gave generously to the poor and prayed regularly to God."

10. Your generosity always provides immediate benefits with a guaranteed return.

Generosity not only gives you a guaranteed future ... it provides immediate returns on your investments.

Ecclesiastes 11:1 in The Message says:

"Be generous: Invest in acts of charity. Charity yields high returns."

11. When you're generous God will make available to you the only bank that will never default or be taken over by the government.

Luke 12:33 in The Message says:

"Be generous. Give to the poor. Get yourselves a bank that can't go bankrupt, a bank in heaven far from bankrobbers, safe from embezzlers, a bank you can bank on. It's obvious, isn't it? The place where your treasure is, is the place you will most want to be, and end up being."

12. Your generosity also has a long-term value greater than any 401K plan or investment.

2 Corinthians 9:9 in the New Living Translation says:

"They share freely and give generously to the poor. Their good deeds will be remembered forever."

If you want your deeds remembered in heaven ... then you must be a generous giver.

THE CYRUS ANOINTING

And by the way, be happy in your generous giving … God loves a cheerful giver.

2 Corinthians 9:7 in the Amplified Bible says:

"Let each one [give] as he has made up his own mind and purposed in his heart, not reluctantly or sorrowfully or under compulsion, for God loves (He takes pleasure in, prizes above other things, and is unwilling to abandon or to do without) a cheerful (joyous, 'prompt to do it') giver [whose heart is in his giving]."

The Message translation of 2 Corinthians 9:6-7 provides even greater insight:

"Remember: A stingy planter gets a stingy crop; a lavish planter gets a lavish crop. I want each of you to take plenty of time to think it over, and make up your own mind what you will give. That will protect you against sob stories and arm-twisting. God loves it when the giver delights in the giving."

When you give what you have in order to put the needs of others above your own … you are blessed with even more.

2 Corinthians 8:1-4 in The Message says:

"Now, friends, I want to report on the surprising

and generous ways in which God is working in the churches in Macedonia province. Fierce troubles came down on the people of those churches, pushing them to the very limit. The trial exposed their true colors: They were incredibly happy, though desperately poor. The pressure triggered something totally unexpected: an outpouring of pure and generous gifts. I was there and saw it for myself. They gave offerings of whatever they could—far more than they could afford!—pleading for the privilege of helping out in the relief of poor Christians."

When you give even in troubled times ... when you do the right thing and bless others, you will even get a bonus.

Ruth 2:11-12 in The Message says:

"Boaz answered her, 'I've heard all about you— heard about the way you treated your mother-in-law after the death of her husband, and how you left your father and mother and the land of your birth and have come to live among a bunch of total strangers. <u>God reward you well for what you've done—and with a generous bonus besides from God</u>, to whom you've come seeking protection under his wings.' "

Key # 5 ...

To the Cyrus Anointing

God Created and Called You for a Specific Purpose.

You may be having the worst year of your life ... you may feel like nothing is going right for you ... but I want you to know ... more importantly, God wants you to know that things can turn around for you immediately ... just like that. (Snap your fingers!)

> Every heartache, every victory, every contact, every mistake overcome, every lesson learned and everything in your life has prepared you for this very moment ... to be used by God for His glory and honor.

Isaiah 45:4 in the New Living Translation says:

"And why have I called you for this work? Why did I call you by name when you did not know me? ..."

The great church leader,
William Barclay:

"There are two great days in a person's life – the day we are born and the day we discover why."

There is something I've noticed on most all tombstones, grave markers or memorial stones. They have the person's name ... the date they were born, a dash, and then the date they passed into eternity.

The dash ... the little mark which represents everything that happens in people's lives between their births and their deaths.

A person is born and they die ... but their life should be more than a dash. We have no control over when we were born and only a certain extent as to when we die. But we do have control over what happens between ... during the dash.

As the Lord brought the dash to my mind, He led

me to James 4:14 which says:

> *"Whereas ye know not what shall be on the morrow. For what is your life? It is even a vapour, that appeareth for a little time, and then vanisheth away."*

There are some people who use this verse to tell you it's not important what you accomplish on this earth ... that life is but a vapor ... here today and gone tomorrow.

Thirty years ago, I had a man tell me he was just a poor soul trying his best to make his way through a troubled world.

The only problem was ... he lived in a colonial mansion that was in an absolute state of disrepair, although he had plenty of money to fix it. He was a retired patent attorney and a shrewd businessman but tighter than words can describe.

At the time I was Director of Development for a Christian college, and this man wouldn't give a penny to Christian education. By the way, he had never married and had one niece who was an Opera singer and needed none of his money.

And if memory serves me correctly ... he sometimes referenced James 4:14.

The key to properly understanding this verse is found in Verses 13 and 15. Here's James 4:14 in context as found in the New Living Translation.

"Look here, you who say, 'Today or tomorrow we are going to a certain town and will stay there a year. We will do business there and make a profit.' How do you know what your life will be like tomorrow? Your life is like the morning fog—it's here a little while, then it's gone. What you ought to say is, 'If the Lord wants us to, we will live and do this or that.' "

The dash that represents our life is best summarized by Verse 15:

"If the Lord wants us to, we will live and do this or that."

Here are seven questions for you to ponder. You need to write down your answers to these questions ... either in the margin of this book or in your electronic data retrieval system or both.

What is it that God wants you to do with your life?

Do you know what His purpose is for you?

> **Do you have a plan for achieving His purpose?**

> **What will be said about you after you're gone?**

> **Will you be missed by your family, friends, acquaintances ... your neighborhood, city, state or nation?**

> **Have you been able to make a difference in the quality of life for others?**

> **Will the fruit of your time on earth remain ... as an inspiration and blessing to others?**

If you were to write your obituary today ... what would it say?

Would you just be a dash ... or a difference maker? Or as Dr. Creflo Dollar would say: "a world changer"?

In fact, I encourage you to write your obituary as if you were dying today. Then I challenge you to write your obituary like you would want it to read ten years from now.

Is there a difference in what it would say today and what it might say in ten years?

If so, what goals do you need to set ... what do you need to accomplish to activate your ten year plan?

Colossians 4:5 in The Message says that we're to:

"... Make the most of every opportunity ..."

That's a good word. In fact, I can tell you that if the dash on your tombstone were just to say that "You Made the Most of Every Opportunity," then Judgment Day would be a glorious experience for you as you would hear Him say:

"Well done thou good and faithful servant."

Your life is more than a vapor ... it is an opportunity for you to fulfill God's purpose and plan for your life ... and that's not a mediocre effort or one of just getting by.

God Has A Purpose For Your Life.

I want you to take a pen and write the following sentence in the margin of this book.

THE CYRUS ANOINTING

God Has a Purpose for My Life.

Now personalize the verse ... for instance, this is how the sentence appears in my book.

God Has a Purpose for Harold Herring's Life.

Purpose gives meaning to WHY you're doing what you're doing. It's time to listen to that inner voice, to give serious attention to what comes naturally to you ... to what gets YOU juiced ... and I don't mean steroids ... to what gets YOU moving at the start of each day.

> **God gave Cyrus a purpose, but He gives you one, too.**

Psalm 18:20-24 in The Message offers some pretty good advice when it says:

"God made my life complete when I placed all the pieces before him. When I got my act together, he gave me a fresh start. Now I'm alert to God's ways; I don't take God for granted. Every day I review the ways he works; I try not to miss a trick. I feel put back together, and I'm watching my step. God rewrote the text of my life when I opened the book of my heart to his eyes."

Key # 6 ...

To the Cyrus Anointing

God Will Raise You Up and Guide Your Actions to Help Set His Children Free.

Isaiah 45:13 in The Message says:

"And now I've got Cyrus on the move. I've rolled out the red carpet before him. He will build my city. He will bring home my exiles. I didn't hire him to do this. I told him."

You're not hearing this teaching by accident ... God stirred me to write it. He wants you to activate the Cyrus Anointing ... which is an anointing to prosper and conquer.

God wants to set you free ... to deliver you from Egypt.

HAROLD HERRING

Do you feel like you have debts that can never be paid?

Do you work under oppressive conditions ... with unsympathetic employers ... while living in a less than desirable neighborhood ... with barely enough food to feed your family and little hope of ever breaking free of what's holding you back?

Welcome to Egypt.

It's important to understand that living in biblical Egypt as the children of Israel did is paralleled to the existence that way too many believers face living in any town in the USA, or in many countries around the world.

However, you can rejoice in knowing that your financial deliverance is coming just as surely as it came to the children of Israel in Egypt.

In order to experience an immediate financial release from the cruel financial taskmasters that you're dealing with ... there are seven keys you need to know.

> **First, you must recognize the ultimate source of your deliverance.**

THE CYRUS ANOINTING

You may have financial advisors ... you may have read every book on getting out of debt, and you may have created a spending plan. All of those things are good ... but the only way you will receive a true and lasting release from financial bondage is when you put your eyes on the ultimate source of your deliverance.

Psalm 25:15 in the New International Version says:

"My eyes are ever on the LORD, for only he will release my feet from the snare."

> **Second, you must recognize that you may have spoken yourself into financial slavery.**

How did you or anyone else get into debt? The answer is ... you spoke yourself into debt.

"Do you have a credit plan?"

"May I open a charge account?"

"Do I get a 10% discount the first time I use my new credit card?"

"What's the maximum amount of time you can finance my new car?"

"What's the smallest down payment I can make on our new home? Also, can we have the closing costs rolled into the amount of the loan?"

The list could go on ... but I think you're familiar on some level with how so many believers have become financial road kill.

Proverbs 6:2 in the Amplified Bible says:

"You are snared with the words of your lips; you are caught by the speech of your mouth."

The New Living Translation of Proverbs 6:2 says:

"... If you have trapped yourself by your agreement and are caught by what you said—"

Now here's the good news found in Proverbs 12:13 in the Amplified Bible which says:

"The wicked is [dangerously] snared by the transgression of his lips, but the [uncompromisingly] righteous shall come out of trouble."

You got yourself into debt by what you said ... you can also get yourself out of debt by what you say.

THE CYRUS ANOINTING

> **Third, ask for forgiveness of your financial mistakes and sin.**

If God were to ask you why you're in debt ... what would you say?

Your answer might be "... because of my car payment or my second car payment or my house payment or my boat payment or my big screen flat panel LCD/LED payment or my vacation payment or my time share payment or my new furniture payment or my credit card payments or department store payments ..."

Are you beginning to see a pattern here?

The two prevalent words that are a part of the debt scenario described in the above paragraph are "my" and "payment."

What would you say if God were to ask you ... did I tell you to buy that stuff or burden yourself with payments? Did you ask me what I thought before signing on the dotted line?

You got yourself into debt, but you're going to need His help to get out.

Acts 26:18 in the Amplified Bible says:

"To open their eyes that they may turn from darkness to light and from the power of Satan to God, so that they may thus receive forgiveness and release from their sins and a place and portion among those who are consecrated and purified by faith in Me."

If I were you ... I'd ask Him now ... if you haven't already.

> **Fourth, will your creditors assist in your release from financial bondage?**

Psalm 144:11 in The Message says:

"Rescue me from the enemy sword, release me from the grip of those barbarians who lie through their teeth, who shake your hand then knife you in the back."

You might wonder if it's fair to characterize your creditors as barbarians. Let's see.

Do credit card companies reveal up front the dangers of using their cards, or do they lure you with seductive ads and the illusion of the lifestyles of the rich and famous just by using their cards?

Are your creditors your best friends as long as you make your payments on time?

Are they offering you the opportunity to skip your payments in November and December so you can have more money for Christmas?

Do they tell you that if you skip those monthly payments during the holiday season that the interest will continue to accumulate and at an even faster rate?

Do the credit barbarians warn you up front about the consequences if you can't make your monthly payments because you were laid off?

Will the people who sold you that new car ... even with your bad credit ... allow you to keep the car while you're looking for a new job?

Credit barbarians are, at best, fair-weather friends, and they're not going to lift a finger to facilitate your release from financial bondage ... but God will. His mercies are renewed daily.

> **Fifth, the only way you'll ever be released from financial bondage is by asking the Ultimate Source for His assistance.**

Jeremiah 29:12-14 in the Amplified Bible says:

"Then you will call upon Me, and you will come and pray to Me, and I will hear and heed you. Then you will seek Me, inquire for, and require Me [as a vital necessity] and find Me when you search for Me with all your heart. I will be found by you, says the Lord, and I will release you from captivity ..."

If you want to avoid a catastrophic financial 9/11 in your life ... it's time for you to make a financial 9-1-1 call to your Heavenly Father.

When you call ... He always answers ... you're one of His favorites.

Psalm 86:7 in The Message says:

"Every time I'm in trouble I call on you, confident that you'll answer."

> **Sixth, God will release you from captivity and give you more than you had before.**

Jeremiah 30:3 in the Amplified Bible says:

"For, note well, the days are coming, says the

THE CYRUS ANOINTING

Lord, when I will release from captivity My people Israel and Judah, says the Lord, and I will cause them to return to the land that I gave to their fathers, and they will possess it."

If you were blessed by this scripture ... you're going to love Zechariah 9:11 in The Message:

"And you, because of my blood covenant with you, I'll release your prisoners from their hopeless cells. Come home, hope-filled prisoners! This very day I'm declaring a double bonus—everything you lost returned twice-over ..."

Hallelujah!!!

"This very day I'm declaring a double bonus ..."

Are you ready for a double bonus?

> **Seventh, your immediate financial release from the bondage of debt is at hand.**

Exodus 14:13 in the New International Version:

"... Do not be afraid. Stand firm and you will see the deliverance the LORD will bring you today.

The Egyptians you see today you will never see again."

This is going to make you shout:

> **The Egyptians (your debtors) you see today ...**
> **... you will never see again.**

> **The mortgage Egyptian you see today ...**
> **... you will never see again.**

> **The credit card Egyptian you see today ...**
> **... you will never see again.**

> **The personal loan Egyptian you see today ...**
> **... you will never see again.**

Why are these true? Because your deliverance from financial suffering ... is coming TODAY.

Is there anything you have to do in the battle for your financial freedom? Just follow the words of 2 Chronicles 20:17 in the New International Version which say:

"You will not have to fight this battle. Take up your positions; stand firm and see the deliver-

*ance the LORD will give you, Judah and Jerusa-
lem. Do not be afraid; do not be discouraged. Go
out to face them tomorrow, and the LORD will be
with you."*

Not only is the Lord with you ... but He will never
fail you.

Deuteronomy 31:6 in the New Living Translation
says:

*"So be strong and courageous! Do not be afraid
and do not panic before them. For the Lord your
God will personally go ahead of you. He will neither fail you nor abandon you."*

Child of God, you are a part of the remnant and
as such are included in the promise of Zechariah 8:12
in the New Living Translation which says:

"For I am planting seeds of peace and prosperity
among you. The grapevines will be heavy with
fruit. The earth will produce its crops, and the
heavens will release the dew. Once more I will
cause the remnant in Judah and Israel to inherit
these blessings."

> **Now it's time to stop acting like
> a slave and begin enjoying
> your financial freedom.**

In 2 Timothy 3:16-17 in the Amplified Bible, you find what I consider to be basic training for your assignment to set the captives free.

> *"Every Scripture is God-breathed (given by His inspiration) and profitable for instruction, for reproof and conviction of sin, for correction of error and discipline in obedience, [and] for training in righteousness (in holy living, in conformity to God's will in thought, purpose, and action), so that the man of God may be complete and proficient, well fitted and thoroughly equipped for every good work."*

This would be a great time to shout ...

... HALLELUJAH!!!

Key # 7 ...

To the Cyrus Anointing

God Will Restore What the Enemy Has Taken From You.

God will use you to help restore everything that has been stolen from His children.

Ezra 6:5 says:

"And also let the golden and silver vessels of the house of God, which Nebuchadnezzar took forth out of the Temple which is at Jerusalem, and brought unto Babylon, be restored, and brought again unto the Temple which is at Jerusalem, everyone to his place, and place them in the house of God."

Everything that the enemy has stolen from you ... God wants it returned.

The income you lost from your job ... He wants it returned to you.

The money that disappeared from your retirement and investment portfolio ... He wants it returned to you.

The profit from your business that was lost during the recession ... He wants it returned to you.

Proverbs 6:31 in the Amplified Bible says:

"But if he is found out [the thief], he must restore seven times [what he stole]; he must give the whole substance of his house [if necessary—to meet his fine]."

I encourage you to make a list of everything the enemy has ever stolen from you.

Multiply the total by seven and begin praising God for the sevenfold restoration of all the enemy has stolen from you.

THE CYRUS ANOINTING

King Cyrus had an anointing to prosper ... God used him ... to set the captives free and as an instrument to return everything that had been stolen from God's children.

As I was writing this teaching ... I sensed in my spirit that God is calling you to operate in the Cyrus Anointing. He is waiting to take you beyond your previous experience and move you into a supernatural realm beyond your wildest expectation.

I'm also sensing that He wants to bring supernatural abundance into your life so that you can ... in turn ... bless others ... who will then glorify God for His goodness.

Cyrus did what God told him to do ... he went where God told him to go ... He gave what God told him to give.

What is God telling you to do ... where is God telling you to go ... what is God telling you to give?

> **I believe that those who receive, activate and operate in the Cyrus Anointing will also function in the end-time office of the Giver.**

Romans 12:6-8 in the New Living Translation says:

> *"In his grace, God has given us different gifts for doing certain things well. So if God has given you the ability to prophesy, speak out with as much faith as God has given you.*

> *"If your gift is serving others, serve them well. If you are a teacher, teach well. If your gift is to encourage others, be encouraging. If it is giving, give generously. If God has given you leadership ability, take the responsibility seriously. And if you have a gift for showing kindness to others, do it gladly."*

Paul is telling us that special people will be divinely empowered to function in supernatural ways of ministry. Paul mentions the functions they will be empowered to perform. He says some will prophesy ... some serve others ... or teach or exhort.

Paul also speaks of an office or function that has never before been activated. He says there will be some specially anointed people who will bring forth large amounts of money into the kingdom of God.

Those who Paul speaks of as holding the office of givers will give exceeding abundantly more than they can even ask or think. After this office, he also mentions others who will rule, and those who will show mercy.

Six of these seven divinely empowered officers have existed in the church since the earliest days. However, the Office of the Supernatural Giver has never before functioned in the church ... at least not in the way I see it in my spirit.

But now, in these last days, as the wealth of the wicked is about to be transferred into the hands of some of God's children, this great office is finally being activated.

Proverbs 13:22 says:

"... The wealth of the sinner is laid up for the just."

Job 27:16, 17 (paraphrased) says:

"... though (wicked men) heap up silver as dust yet the innocent shall divide the silver."

Ecclesiastes 2:26 says:

"... to the sinner (God) giveth travail to gather and to heap up that he may give it to him that is

good before God ..."

> **I firmly believe the Office of the Giver and the Cyrus Anointing go hand-in-hand.**

Pray this prayer and ask God if He wants you to function in these end-time anointings.

How Not to Activate the Cyrus Anointing

You can't buy the anointing ... it's not for sale.

Never has been ... never will be.

You've never seen a late-night infomercial offering the anointing for only three easy payments of $39.99. Though I will admit there are folks who seem to package the anointing as if it were a product for sale ... but once again ... it's not.

Acts 8:18 in the Amplified Bible says:

"However, when Simon saw that the [Holy] Spirit was imparted through the laying on of the apostles' hands, he brought money and offered it to them."

Simon made two mistakes ...

Well, maybe three ...

> **First, he coveted the gifting that was in Peter and the other disciples.**

> **Second, he didn't understand or even want to understand how the anointing worked ... he just wanted it for himself.**

Acts 8:19 in the Amplified Bible says:

"Saying, Grant me also this power and authority, in order that anyone on whom I place my hands may receive the Holy Spirit."

> **Third, his ignorance of the anointing and of the men who were manifesting the gifts ... caused him to think it was for sale, when, in fact, it was not.**

Simon saw the demonstration of power ... and he wanted it. He gave no consideration to or showed any interest in learning the source of the power.

THE CYRUS ANOINTING

Acts 8:20 in the Amplified Bible says:

"But Peter said to him, Destruction overtake your money and you, because you imagined you could obtain the [free] gift of God with money!"

When you want to do a right thing ... healing the sick ... setting the Captives free ... for a wrong reason ... it will lead to trouble ... in fact, more trouble than you want to handle or deal with.

Acts 8:21 in the Amplified Bible says:

"You have neither part nor lot in this matter, for your heart is all wrong in God's sight [it is not straightforward or right or true before God]."

The New Living Translation of Acts 8:21 says:

"You can have no part in this, for your heart is not right with God."

> **If your heart is not right with God ... then you will not be a vessel anointed and appointed for His use.**

There are some well-meaning Christians who get this verse and this passage confused.

When I write partners a monthly letter ... I'm teaching them the Word of God ... plus I'm allowing them the opportunity to plant seed in good ground.

The reason for the seed-sowing is simple ... if you don't sow you won't reap. Yet, a few say, sowers are trying to buy the gifts and blessings of God ... that's simply not true.

Sowers give because they understand the principles of seedtime and harvest as outlined in Genesis 8:22 which says:

"While the earth remaineth, seedtime and harvest, and cold and heat, and summer and winter, and day and night shall not cease."

Seedtime and harvest will follow one another ... just as surely as night follows day ... and winter follows summer.

If seedtime and harvest are a part of God's order ... then we should teach them every time the opportunity arises.

Also, Galatians 6:7 in the Amplified Bible says:

"Do not be deceived and deluded and misled; God will not allow Himself to be sneered at (scorned, disdained, or mocked by mere preten-

sions or professions, or by His precepts being set aside.) [He inevitably deludes himself who attempts to delude God.] For whatever a man sows, that and that only is what he will reap."

What you sow ... you will reap ... it's that simple.

But Simon's problem was that he didn't know the Word ... he didn't have any sort of personal relationship with God ... so he thought the anointing was something you purchased.

Always remember ...

... you can't have the gift without knowing the giver.

Acts 8:22-23 in the Amplified Bible says:

"So repent of this depravity and wickedness of yours and pray to the Lord that, if possible, this contriving thought and purpose of your heart may be removed and disregarded and forgiven you. For I see that you are in the gall of bitterness and in a bond forged by iniquity [to fetter souls]."

The real depravity and wickedness in Simon's heart is very simple. If you accept Jesus as your Lord and Savior ... then you're free of all your sin.

Pray to the Lord and He will forgive you.

Acts 8:24 in the Amplified Bible says:

"And Simon answered, Pray for me [beseech the Lord, both of you], that nothing of what you have said may befall me!"

Regardless of what you have done in the past ... you can be forgiven, allowing you to move on with your life and your plans for now and eternity.

Isaiah 43:25 in the Amplified Bible says:

"I, even I, am He Who blots out and cancels your transgressions, for My own sake, and I will not remember your sins."

The Message translation of Isaiah 43:25 says:

"But I, yes I, am the one who takes care of your sins—that's what I do. I don't keep a list of your sins."

I think we've clearly established that the anointing and gifts of God are not for sale ... at any price. However, they're free and available to every born again believer.

THE CYRUS ANOINTING

One more thing ... the anointing of God is transferrable not by birthright but by the actions and attitudes of your heart.

No parent ... no matter how spiritual or high profile their ministry may be ... can automatically transfer their anointing to a sibling ... if things don't line up in their lives.

Now that we have discussed how not to receive and activate the Cyrus or any other anointing ... let's talk about how you can activate the anointing.

How to Activate the Cyrus Anointing Right Now

Anointings are transferrable ... when your heart is right ... and when you OBEY THE WORD.

Elijah transferred the anointing that was on him to Elisha.

2 Kings 2:8-10 says:

"And Elijah took his mantle, and wrapped it together, and smote the waters, and they were divided hither and thither, so that they two went over on dry ground.

"And it came to pass, when they were gone over, that Elijah said unto Elisha, Ask what I shall do for thee, before I be taken away from thee. And Elisha said, I pray thee, let a double portion of thy spirit be upon me.

"And he said, Thou hast asked a hard thing: nevertheless, if thou see me when I am taken from thee, it shall be so unto thee; but if not, it shall not be so."

First, you have to recognize the anointing you want.

Elisha recognized the anointing on Elijah because he traveled with him.

Elisha wasn't just a face in the crowed ... Elisha served Elijah in order to facilitate his ministry and to attend to his comforts as they traveled.

Elisha was an understudy ... but yet he was also a personal valet.

During this time of service to the prophet ... Elisha repeatedly saw the power of God manifesting through Elijah.

For years, Kenneth Copeland carried the briefcase of Dr. Oral Roberts. He served him with joy and honor. There came a time when he picked up his mantle of healing and prosperity.

Even though Brother John Avanzini, my personal friend and mentor, prayed over me and transferred the

THE CYRUS ANOINTING

Debt Free Anointing on his life into mine ... I still served him wherever we went and whatever we did. It was ... and still is to this very day ... a matter of honor.

As long as he draws breath on planet earth ... I will be attentive to his every need and desire.

That's how Elisha treated Elijah ... because he recognized and honored the anointing on his life.

> **Second, you have to realize that the anointing is not a trophy to put on a shelf ... but a gifting to be used for His glory.**

2 Kings 2:8 says:

"And Elijah took his mantle, and wrapped it together, and smote the waters, and they were divided hither and thither, so that they two went over on dry ground."

Some people want the anointing to say ... look at me ... see what I've got ... I must be somebody special.

A truly anointed person recognizes why they have the anointing and what it's for. They're also willing to pay the price ... to use that anointing for His glory.

HAROLD HERRING

Yes, I walk in the Debt Free Anointing ... but my obedience to His direction has lead me to do 500 meetings in five years.

I remember where I was at ... when God told me He wanted me to start doing meetings during the week. He told me He wanted me to go where He told me to go ... to never worry about how many people were in the audience and to always be the last one to leave.

Sometimes there were travel delays, bad weather, small crowds and smaller offerings ... but I was never discouraged ... because I knew I was fulfilling the calling and anointing that was on my life.

I remember one time asking God why He was sending me to Salt Lake City. In a city where over 95% of the people are Mormons ... and where we have a small database ... He directed me to hold a meeting.

I will always remember ... the night of the meeting there were 54 people present ... 20 of whom were pastors. Then I understood why God sent me there ... He wanted me to encourage and help those pastors.

For over ten years, we lived on the tenth hole of a golf course. I only played golf on that course four times in all those years. I like golf ... but I had a higher calling.

THE CYRUS ANOINTING

As you move into the Cyrus Anointing ... be ready to go where God says to go and do what He says to do.

> **Third, you have to ask for the anointing.**

God showed me He is READY TO GIVE YOU the Cyrus Anointing, but you have to ask for it.

He says that YOU CAN HAVE IT if you really want it!

Regardless of his past service, his loyalty or attention to duty ... there came a point where Elisha had to ask for a double portion of the anointing that was on Elijah.

Let's look at 2 Kings 2:9:

"And it came to pass, when they were gone over, that Elijah said unto Elisha, Ask what I shall do for thee ... And Elisha said, I pray thee, let a double portion of thy spirit be upon me."

I am convinced that God is saying the very same thing to you right now! He wants to give you the Cyrus Anointing, but you must ask for it.

John 14:13-14 says it pretty clearly.

"And whatsoever ye shall ask in my name, that will I do ... If ye shall ask anything in my name, I will do it."

Matthew 7:7-8 has a very important message you need to get down in your spirit.

"Ask, and it shall be given you; seek, and ye shall find; knock, and it shall be opened unto you:

"For every one that asketh receiveth; and he that seeketh findeth; and to him that knocketh it shall be opened."

Notice there is no asterisk in the second part that says "everyone" includes everyone but you. God's benefits are for you, too.

God wants you to walk in the Cyrus Anointing, but you must ask.

Remember the words of James 4:2 which say:

"... you do not have, because you do not ask."

You need to ask.

THE CYRUS ANOINTING

> **Fourth, you have to want it
> more than anything else.**

How badly do you want the Cyrus Anointing?

You have to want it more than television ... more than surfing the internet ... more than time hanging out with your friends ... more than playing or watching your favorite sports teams ... you've got to want it as much as the air you breathe.

Once a young man came to Socrates and said, "I want to learn everything you know. I want your wisdom."

To that Socrates responded, "Follow me to that river. Take a close look and tell me what you see."

The young man replied, "I see only the river, of course."

Socrates told him to peep down into the water and look closer.

As he leaned closer, Socrates grabbed the man's head and shoved it under water!!!

The man tried to escape and flailed his arms

wildly as he choked.

But Socrates' strong grip kept his head submerged in water just a little more time!

As the young man continued to struggle, finally Socrates released his grip and let his head come out of water.

"Are you crazy, old man? You want to kill me?" shouted the young man, gasping for his breath.

Socrates asked him, "When I was holding your head underwater, what is the one thing you needed most? What did you want more than anything else?"

"I wanted to breathe. I wanted air, of course," said the man, still panting.

"So," Socrates said, "if and when you want WISDOM that badly, like you wanted AIR, then you come to me!!!"

When you want the Cyrus Anointing activated in your life more than anything else ... more than life itself ...

... it will activate.

THE CYRUS ANOINTING

Fifth, you have to realize that it may not be easy.

2 Kings 2:10 says:

"And he said, Thou hast asked a hard thing: nevertheless, if thou see me when I am taken from thee, it shall be so unto thee; but if not, it shall not be so."

Why did Elijah say it was difficult? Because he knew that Elisha could choose to listen to all the negative folks.

You know the kind of people he was talking about. They ask ... Why do you read your Bible? Why do you tithe and give offerings? Why do you believe in the prayer of faith?

Elijah knew that Elisha had a choice to make ... he could listen to all the negative people around him or he could choose to believe the Man of God.

You face those choices every day. You can choose to listen to the people who knew you B.C. (Before Christ) or you can choose a new set of friends, those who will encourage, exhort and edify you.

You will either be blessed or cursed by your

associations and the people you listen to.

1 Corinthians 15:33 in the Amplified Bible says:

"Do not be so deceived and misled! Evil companionships (communion, associations) corrupt and deprave good manners and morals and character."

Proverbs 13:20 in The Message says:

"Become wise by walking with the wise; hang out with fools and watch your life fall to pieces."

Do not hang out with or allow into your inner circle people who are content with their debt, troubled or live a just-get-by way of life.

If you want to get out of debt ... then you need to associate with people who have already gotten out of debt or come alongside those who are taking the steps necessary to gain financial freedom.

The friend who thinks it's funny that his third car is about to be repossessed will not be encouraging when you're paying off your car early.

The friend who's afraid to make a decision ... will not be a good example in making wise investment choices.

THE CYRUS ANOINTING

The friend who gets career advice from the person who was fired because of incompetence will never rise to the top of the business ladder.

The woman who says she'll never get out of debt because her family has always been in debt will not understand the out-of-debt plan you've developed for your life.

Relax. I'm not telling you to abandon your friends or family ... but I'm telling you some facts. Like produces like. Your attitude, speech and behavior are all directly affected by the people you spend a lot of time with.

If you're committed to elevating your life ... then add some new friends. Hang around folks who have it together ... personally and financially.

Make no mistake about it ... you are blessed or cursed by your associations.

As you walk in the Cyrus Anointing, expand your circle of friends who understand your calling and support you.

> **Sixth, you have to be continually observant.**

2 Kings 2:10 says:

"... nevertheless, if thou see me when I am taken from thee, it shall be so unto thee; but if not, it shall not be so."

The best way to learn is to look, listen and ask. When you have shown yourself faithful ... observing to do all things commanded of you ... then blessings will follow.

Consider the story of Elizabeth and Zechariah ... found in Luke 1:5-6 in the New International Version which says:

> *"In the time of Herod king of Judea there was a priest named Zechariah, who belonged to the priestly division of Abijah; his wife Elizabeth was also a descendant of Aaron. Both of them were righteous in the sight of God, observing all the Lord's commands and decrees blamelessly."*

Pay particular attention to Verse 6 which says that Zechariah and Elizabeth were righteous in the sight of God, observing all the Lord's commands and decrees blamelessly.

Because they carefully observed and obeyed God's instructions, they were blessed.

THE CYRUS ANOINTING

Luke 1:7 goes on to say:

"But they were childless because Elizabeth was not able to conceive, and they were both very old."

Their observant obedience was honored. Luke 1:13-15 still in the New International Version says:

"But the angel said to him: 'Do not be afraid, Zechariah; your prayer has been heard. Your wife Elizabeth will bear you a son, and you are to call him John. He will be a joy and delight to you, and many will rejoice because of his birth.' "

Make it your business to observe everything you can from others who operate in an anointing similar to yours. You don't want to be them or respond as they do ... but through observation ... God can reveal even deeper truths to you.

> **Seventh, once you receive the anointing you must use it.**

God would never give you an ability unless He expected you to use it.

2 Kings 2:13-14 says:

"He took up also the mantle of Elijah that fell

from him, and went back, and stood by the bank of Jordan;

"And he took the mantle of Elijah that fell from him, and smote the waters, and said, Where is the LORD God of Elijah? and when he also had smitten the waters, they parted hither and thither: and Elisha went over."

Just as Elisha assumed the double portion anointing of Elijah, I encourage you to demonstrate the anointing you're walking under.

This demonstration should in no way be prideful but rather beneficial to all who surround you. It's important that you use what you've got ... right where you are.

One of the most powerful men of God in modern day Church history was Dwight L. Moody. I was reading about Dwight L. Moody. Did you know he flunked church membership class twice in a row? One time, after preaching, the deacon board called him to the side and corrected him, saying, "Brother Moody, you massacre the queen's English." (He was a very uneducated man.)

Brother Moody, about whom history records that, even without mass media, he eventually won over one million souls to the Lord, replied to those who criticized his ignorant use of the English language, "I'm doing the best I can with all I have right now. What are you doing with what you have?"

That's the real question: What are you doing with what you have? It's when you take what you have and you give it to God that He's able to go into tomorrow and make provisions available for your next step.

One other thing: If there is hidden sin in your life, Satan will use it to overthrow you. Hidden sin makes it easy for him to take your goods.

When you find sin in your life, go immediately to Jesus and ask for forgiveness. As soon as you do this, the devil loses his ability to steal from you. It is as simple as praying this prayer in 1 John 1:9:

> "If we confess our sins, he is faithful and just to forgive us our sins, and to cleanse us from all unrighteousness."

Prayer of Release for the Cyrus Anointing

Heavenly Father, I have not because I ask not. So I'm asking on this ___ day of _____ (month) _____ (year) for the end-time Cyrus Anointing to be released into my life.

Through your Word I have been shown how to release my faith and to act upon your Word when it's heard in my heart (rhema) and acted upon in my life (logos).

I'm touching my eyes to see things I've never seen before ... beyond my natural vision. I'm asking to see things with the eyes of the spirit ... and the heart of faith.

I'm touching my ears to hear things that I've never heard before ... the voice of the Spirit as it directs me to opportunities and possibilities beyond human comprehension.

I'm touching the temples of my head to gain wisdom

and understanding beyond the natural mind ... anything that I previously understood or had knowledge of.

I'm praying for the mind of Christ that's in me to function fully and freely every moment of the day.

I'm touching the palms of my hands ... as you have given me the power ... the ability to get wealth ... to bless others.

I'm touching my throat ... to ordain that the words coming out of my mouth are not born of my flesh but rather birthed in my spirit. I will use the words of my mouth as a creative force to improve the quality of life for every person I meet.

Heavenly Father, I decree and declare right now that the Cyrus Anointing is released into my life.

I decree and declare that financial miracles will manifest in the life of every person I meet.

I decree and declare that I will be faithful in my tithes and offerings, that I will stay in faith and live in positive expectancy for the activation of every promise in your Word.

I decree and declare that I'm a vessel of honor ready to become a part of the end-time wealth transfer into the hands of the children of God.

I decree and declare that a financial anointing will flow through my life into the lives of those I meet.

I decree and declare that I will faithfully execute the seven keys of the Cyrus Anointing as long as there is life in my body.

I decree and declare that I will honor His Presence, His house and His Word. (Key #1)

I decree and declare that I will position myself to be equipped by God for the heavenly vision He has stirred in me. (Key #2)

I decree and declare that I'm strengthened in knowledge that God will go before me protecting me and defeating my enemies. (Key #3)

I decree and declare that I will allow God to direct my path to hidden treasures and secret riches. (Key #4)

I decree and declare that I will fulfill the specific purpose for which I was created, putting aside all excuses. (Key #5)

I decree and declare that I will allow God to guide my steps, direct my path and lead me in the way He would have me go. (Key #6)

I decree and declare a seven-fold restoration of everything the enemy has ever taken from me. (Key #7)

Finally, Lord, I decree and declare that I'm committing all that's within me and everything you can move through me to be a faithful partaker of the Cyrus Anointing.

Lord, I witness my name to this declaration of the Cyrus Anointing in my life.

_____

(Sign Your Name)

Hallelujah, the Cyrus Anointing has been released into your life.

I want to know that you've taken up the mantle of the end-time Cyrus Anointing.

Complete the Cyrus Anointing Declaration on the next page and mail it to me so that I can join you in a powerful prayer of release.

You may also notify me by going to:

debtfreearmy.org/cyrus anointing

Cyrus Anointing Declaration

Thank you, Brother Harold, for your time and investment in me. I have chosen to take up the mantle of the end-time Cyrus Anointing in my life, and I want you to know.

Praise God, and may he continue his work in you!

Your Name:

_____

Additional Information You
Wish to Provide:

_____

_____

_____

Mail to:

The Debt Free Army
P.O. Box 900000
Fort Worth, Texas
76161

7 Keys to Activating

The Cyrus Anointing

Invite Harold Herring to speak at your church, event, or rally.

Would you like to invite Harold to be a guest speaker at your church, event, or rally? Just send an email to:

booking@haroldherring.com

or call 1-800-583-2963

With a mix of humor, practical strategies, and Biblical insight Harold will inspire, encourage, and prepare you to change your financial destiny and set you on the path to not only set you free from debt but keep you free of debt and living the debt free life God has called you to.

Keep Thinking Rich Thoughts,

Harold Herring